IT'S NOT
ROCKET
SCIENCE

TIPS TO EDUCATE BLACK & BROWN BOYS

IT'S NOT ROCKET SCIENCE

TIPS TO EDUCATE BLACK & BROWN BOYS

NATE HIGGINS

MILESTONE
PUBLISHING HOUSE

Published by Milestone Publishing House, Dallas/Fort Worth, Texas.

Cover & Interior Design by Roy Roper, wideyedesign.net

ISBN-10: 0-9862052-0-6
ISBN-13: 978-0-9862052-0-0
Printed in the USA

SPECIAL THANKS

I would like to thank all of the doctors who have influenced and protected me:

- Dr. Lorraine Monroe, you are the reason I am an educator today. You took a 13-year-old boy from Harlem and helped make me a man. Your vision lives on.

- Dr. Lonnetta Gaines, thank you for being my unofficial aunt and helping to sustain LMLI for many years. Yes, I Can Imagine!

- Dr. Claytisha Walden, you pushed me and gave me the ability and confidence to hone my skills.

- To my mother and granny, thank you for raising a man.

- To the Blue Team, thank you for inspiring and pushing me. I love you. Blue Team Go!

- To Paloma, the sky's the limit. Thank you for helping me to see that.

- To my brothers and my sister, Ray, Rey, Darryl, D, Gary, Jason, Elijah, and Jessica, you guys have stood by me through it all. I love you.

DEDICATION

This book is dedicated to my family.

Our journey never ends, but together we can do it all.

I love you.

To every educator who has impacted my life.

THANK YOU.

CONTENTS

INTRODUCTION

I wrote this book, because as an educator and administrator, I saw that there was a void that needed to be filled. There are many teachers who view their black and brown boy students as the main cause of their problems with classroom management. They look at this particular demographic of student and act as if they can't handle or teach them. I have had countless conversations with teachers who struggled with classroom management, particularly with their black and brown boy students, who were summarily amazed at how I as well as other educators made classroom management look easy. It was as if they felt there was a magic wand, somehow hidden from them that I waved over my students to get them fully engaged and wanting to learn. Some even equated it to race, but I would show them a teacher who was not the same race as the black and brown boys they taught and whose management was equal to or better than mine. Still others equated it to age, but I would show them teachers of all ages doing what they had previously felt was impossible. One day a teacher asked me "So, Mr. Higgins what's the magic trick or magic answer?" I simply replied, "It's not rocket science." They laughed and said that one day they hoped I would reveal my secret to them. So, I began to share with them so they could implement the strategies you are about to read. After a few months, they started to see more and more progress – and finally success.

If a magic wand exists, I think we all have one! Hopefully this book will help you to realize that with a few strategies, you can educate and improve the lives of all of your students – even your black and brown boys.

In this book, you will notice that I make references to gangs. In no way do I support gangs or gang activity; having seen the negative effects of gangs and gang violence firsthand, I know well the destruction they cause. What I am examining is how they manage to capture and affect the lives of so many black and brown boys. Gang leaders have found ways to recruit and engage black and brown boys for wrongdoing. Let's take what they use negatively and instead use it to influence our boys in a positive and meaningful way.

In this book, you will also notice my reference to coaches and what they do with their black and brown athletes. Oftentimes, these athletes are the same students you teach, the students who you feel you cannot get through to. Why is this? Having been an athlete in high school and college, I have learned many different things about teamwork, education, and strategy and can even still execute some basketball plays I learned way back in high school. Many lower income students throughout the U.S. are star athletes at different schools, at different levels; Why is this?

In my experience, some of the plays and strategies developed by coaches are just as complicated as many algebraic or scientific problems, yet these athletes, who are also considered your problem students, execute them to perfection.

As a teacher, you must learn to tap into the strategies that these groups – gangs and coaches – use in order to reach your students. We will review some of these strategies in the interest of overall student success and see how we can relate them to your classroom practices.

"You can't lead the people, if you don't love the people.

You can't save the people, if you don't serve the people."

CORNELL WEST

CHAPTER 1
C.A.R.E. — CHALLENGE, ASSERT, REINFORCE, ENGAGE

I am often surprised at the large number of people who think that black and brown boys can't learn or can't be taught. If we look at those who dominate most inner-city gangs and most organized sports, we will see overwhelmingly that they are these same black and brown boys. In both cases these boys are being led by someone. Most inner-city gangs have an organizational structure similar in many ways to that of a Fortune 500 company. What seems like unorganized chaos is actually structured very carefully. There are a few at the top living very well and many more at the bottom striving to attain the lifestyle that those at the top already have. Sports teams are led or run by a coach or owner. In many cases, at the top levels, these coaches and owners do not look like the players of which they lead. So, how are they successful in getting through to these athletes in order to lead them to victory?

Having played organized sports in high school, as well as college; and having experienced gang recruitment and violence, I realized that both of these groups had leaders who followed a very similar format. For the purposes of this book, I have summed it up with the acronym C.A.R.E., which stands for: Challenge, Assert, Reinforce, and Engage. I know you are wondering how I can reasonably use the word "CARE" while talking about gang leaders. However, as you journey with me, you will better understand that in the eyes of black and brown boys, they actually portray quite well both what the word means and what the acronym stands for.

Gangs flourish because they create a false sense of community and give troubled kids something to belong to. The ultimate goal, of course, is for the low-level gangbangers to secure territory, helping to provide a small financial gain for themselves and a much greater financial gain for the higher-ups. Coaches show they CARE by maintaining a certain level of discipline and, in some cases, making their players feel like they are family and helping them explore sports as a way to a more success-ful life. There is a reason why most coaches bond so closely with their players. One thing we all need to realize is that coaches are TEACHERS.

They teach players to hone their skills both in the sport that the coach teaches and in life. I still live many of the principles that were instilled in me by my high school basketball coach. This is not by accident: it works in the same way many top gang leaders act as teachers (though, of course, not in the same positive manner). They have both figured out a way to show that they CARE in order to reach their ultimate goals. Let's examine how we can use the acronym C.A.R.E. in the classroom.

C- Challenge

A- Assert

R- Reinforce

E- Engage

C- CHALLENGE

In the classroom, we have to always challenge our black and brown boys to be the best students they can be. We have to push them academically to go beyond what they imagine they can accomplish. If we believe, they ultimately will believe - and do. They are challenged every day by the many negative stereotypes society feeds them. They are also challenged every day by their peers and neighborhoods. They are constantly being force-fed negative images and encouraged to engage in underachieving lifestyles.

In terms of classroom management, if you can smartly and academically challenge your black and brown boys, you've won half the battle. What, though, does it mean to challenge your students "smartly and academically"? Well, that depends quite a lot on both the subject you teach and the level at which you teach. If you have black and brown boy students who are below grade level or who can't perform to the requisite level in your subject area, you have to first identify their shortcomings and then attack their deficiencies with both vigor and a certain amount of CARE. This demonstrates to them that you are there to teach them and that you intend to continue to challenge them to be their best. It can be implemented by effectively differentiating instruction, extra tutoring, gentle prompting, and anything else you feel your particular boys need to bring them up to the proper level.

What about challenging your students in order to show dominance in the classroom? This may be needed, and it looks different for different teachers and classrooms. I do know one thing; all students, no matter what color, age, or race, can detect weakness and will ultimately embrace dominance. We can all relate to the love and respect we have for our favorite teachers or coaches, and at some point they challenged us and pushed us to be our best. In many classrooms, especially in urban neighborhoods, I have noticed there is that one boy or group of black and brown boys who are generally dominant. Coaches realize this on the playing field or court, and they tend to challenge that big, bad athlete in order to demonstrate both to that athlete and to the rest of the team that they, the coaches, are really in charge. The challenge is usually mental rather than physical; the coach challenges the athlete to a task in which they show that player that they are not up to par and then the coach demonstrates that he has a better way to compete. From that challenge the athletes realize that they need the coach. This realization comes mainly out of embarrassment, but something clicks in their brain and they know at that moment that this person is their best chance of getting better. In the classroom there will always be that challenge by students, especially black and brown boys, because in most cases they are used to being dominant or they are used to teachers who only pretend to care. They seek out and destroy the pretenders. You must commit to not being destroyed.

My mentor, and the reason I am in education, is herself a world-renowned educator. In her speeches she often tells the story of a black boy who was new to her classroom and who tried to assert his dominance. She was teaching in a New York City public school classroom, and she received a new student from Philadelphia. As she was writing an assignment on the board and instructing the class on what to do, the boy said out loud, "Man, I ain't doing that shit!" This was his moment to try and show his new classroom that he was the bad kid out of Philly and that he would be the dominant student in the classroom. Now my mentor has mastered the art of classroom management. She knew that the kid was trying to test her and that if she reacted wrongly, she would lose the respect of the class. She called the student up to her, and as he slowly walked up to the front of the classroom, she began to write a note. As she was writing, she read the note out loud: "Dear Counselor, I am writing to introduce you to Mr. So and So. He is new to the school and new to my class. He doesn't want to do my shit. Place him in a classroom with another teacher, so he can do their shit." The kid was amazed, and by the time he got up to her he was pleading, "Please, please, Ms. Monroe, I don't want to go anywhere else." Without looking up, she said, "If you can be back in your seat before I look up, we will forget about this incident." What do you think happened? Well, if you've ever heard Dr. Lorraine Monroe speak, you will know that student was back in his seat before she could look up, and he became one of her biggest allies.

There will be many challenges. As educators we must realize why there are challenges and that the way in which we handle those challenges must be composed and must show our students that we are there to support them and help them to learn – especially our black and brown boys.

A – ASSERT

After you have won a challenge, you have to assert your authority and model your plan for success. Black and brown boys will respond to authority once they realize the person in charge is knowledgeable and dominant enough to lead them to success.

Coaches do this when they map out plays or they come up with strategies to win games. They make their athletes practice the plays or strategies they have developed over and over again. This is done to further ingrain within the players the coach's strategy for success. After a coach has challenged his players and has shown that he is dominant, he presents a comprehensive plan that he believes will lead them to success. Athletes follow that plan because they want to win. Coaches teach a team concept where the players act upon what the leader has designed and everyone works towards the same goal.

In the classroom, you must assert your authority through a well-designed educational plan that targets the students' shortcomings so that they can succeed. In creating your plan for black and brown boys, you must take into account the many relevant social and educational factors and ensure that you design something that specifically works in addressing their areas of deficiency. Present it and outline it in such a way that makes it evident to them that following your plan will yield their success. This takes a lot of work and a thorough knowledge of your students. You must be able to examine them and size them up academically in the same way in which a coach sizes up the talent of his athletes and then devises strategies to help them improve. This must be done very early on so that valuable time isn't wasted and your students don't fall further behind.

R - REINFORCE

After you have succeeded at asserting your plan of success in the daily classroom routine, there may come a point at which, as a result of some newfound success, your black and brown boys feel as if they can break away from this plan and begin to do their own thing. This next step is key to ensuring continued future success, both yours and theirs. You have to reinforce your authority. This means to show your students that the success they have gained is not by accident, but rather because of a well-thought-out plan created by you. You need to show them that if they continue with the plan, they will continue to be successful. Handling this step with caution is crucial, because some black and brown boys may get lost if you don't.

When gang members begin to experience success, they may often come back and challenge the leader. A gang leader usually reinforces his authority either by physical abuse or by hurting the rebellious gang member monetarily. When a coach's player wishes to break off from the team's philosophy or begins to run their own plays, the coach usually reminds them that they are a part of a team, and they are often benched, or in some extreme cases, kicked off of the team altogether. In both cases, to get back in their leader's good graces, they have to do more work than their peers in order to re-prove their loyalty.

In the classroom, we can't physically harm our black and brown boys and we can't just kick them out (except in the most extreme cases). One way in which you can reinforce your authority is by reminding them how much more they need to learn. What does that mean, and how does it look in the classroom? You of all people should know your students' areas of weakness and where they need to be strengthened academically for their ultimate success to be assured. So, you now present them with work that will show them where they need to be to reach the next level; they will most likely struggle with this level of work. They will begin to get frustrated, but before things get out of hand and your student shuts down, you must remind them that the plan you have created will have them surpassing this level with the investment of more time and effort on their part. Your black and brown boys may have to have a humbling experience so that they realize they have more work to do before they can be successful.

For some students this strategy may not work. At that point you must re-examine your original plan for success. You may have to take into account some of their suggestions in order to formulate a new plan that gets them to master the curriculum you want them to learn. Then you can incorporate some things they may feel they need help with or just want to learn. These may be things you have not previously considered in a classroom setting.

E - ENGAGE

If you have had any classroom experience with black and brown boys, or any student for that matter, you know that the time in which the most trouble happens is during idle time. Black and brown boys must constantly be engaged; this is why I believe coaches and even gang leaders have a lot of success with them. Obviously, gang leaders keep their members engaged in negative or destructive behavior, but they keep them engaged nonetheless; they know that if a member remains idle too long, they may venture off and possibly do something against the gang leader's wishes. Coaches know that the more their athlete is engaged, the more they are controlling what they are engaged in. This engagement can vary from practicing plays (even to the point of redundancy) to exercising continually in order to stay in good shape. If you have ever watched a practice of any sport, you rarely see athletes idly on the sidelines; in other words, you never see them not being engaged. Similarly, this should never happen in your classroom. This is the one thing I typically see the teachers who struggle the most with classroom management fail to control- their idle time.

With black and brown boys, you have to constantly have them engaged in learning. If you have asserted and reinforced your plan for success, then they should always have something to do; if they don't, it is your plan that is failing. If they have completed their class-related tasks, you need to have some sort of work for them that purposefully challenges their academic shortcomings. When this gets monotonous, one way you can build stronger relationships with them is to have them engaged as helpers in the class. You will be surprised at how the simple task of helping you distribute materials or take a count of students can keep them engaged in learning and feel as if they are important to you. First, engage them academically as much as you can, and then engage them with classroom tasks that can help build leadership characteristics.

One of my coaches used to engage the worst player or the player with the most academic issues more than the others by making him a team captain. As a team captain, you had more responsibility than the other members of the team. You were often the first in the gym or the film room and the last out. You dedicated more of yourself to maintain that status. Later on in life, I realized this was by design, because it kept those players more engaged than the others and it forced them to buy in to the coach's philosophy whole-heartedly. You may be in a classroom with a few black and brown boys, or they may make up the majority of your students. If you keep them engaged academically, you reduce idle time; and if you engage a selected few that struggle more than others with behavior or academic problems, you may be the key to their success.

CARE is something that must be implemented early when dealing with your black and brown boy students. It also stands for more than just an acronym; you must be very genuine with this population of students in order to help them. Some come into your classroom scarred by their backgrounds; they will know if you genuinely CARE for them as well. If you do, they will become some of your biggest allies and will allow you to help them succeed both in the classroom and in life.

"A brain is a brain,

train it."

DR. LORRAINE MONROE

CHAPTER 11

A BRAIN IS A BRAIN — TRAIN IT

I challenge anyone reading this book to go to a medical research facility or a morgue and examine a table full of brains – just brains – and pick out the brain that belongs to a black or brown boy. I challenge you to identify a brain belonging to anyone of any racial background or demographic. If you can do that, I will personally refund to you the cost of this book. It sounds ridiculous – trust me, I know. I am attempting to show you how ridiculous it is when we let one of our black or brown boys fail, because we think their brains work differently.

In essence, a brain is just a brain, but it's how that brain is trained that determines what one ultimately does and accomplishes. According to the 1985 book Principles of Neural Development by Dale Purves and

Jeff Lichtman, "The brain does not simply grow, but rather develops in an intricately orchestrated sequence of stages." There are physical and mental stages of growth as well as factors that affect each. If we are trained to do something over and over, we naturally become better at that skill. People win spelling bees because of hours and hours of preparation and study. Professional athletes hone their skills by practicing for those same hours upon hours. People who are really good at what they do or those who are specialists in a particular field tend to spend more time honing their skills than others. Yes, natural ability is a factor, but for the most part they have trained their brains and bodies to master their skill.

Many of our black and brown boy students have been trained to do something very well. Some things may be good and some things may not be good, but they have been trained or they have trained their minds and bodies to be good at something. You have to train their brain for academic excellence. It boils my blood when I hear an educator say, "Well, they can't read" or "They just can't learn." Yet, these same black and brown boys can quote rap lyrics or execute plays on the court or field. On the negative side, they can also run and lead gangs, which operate in much the same way as do small businesses. So, good or bad, yes, THEY CAN LEARN. The challenge is – how do YOU teach them? Train their brains for good, uncover how they learn best, and emphasize these things so that they can sharpen their academic skills.

One of my favorite movies is "The Program", which stars James Caan, Halle Berry, Omar Epps, Craig Sheffer and Kristy Swanson. The movie is about a major college football program and shows how several payers deal with the pressure of the competition on and off the field. I reference this because one of the characters, Alvin Mack, is an All-American Linebacker who can barely read or write. He has fallen through the cracks academically and doesn't even attempt to do academic work with his designated college tutor. From what we know of him in the movie, he appears to solely depend on his ability to play football and not on his academic studies to survive. However, there is a scene in which the team is reviewing game film in order to prepare for an upcoming game against a rival. As the defensive leader, the coach is questioning Alvin about plays and what happens if this or that occurs on the football field. Alvin is dead on in his responses. He knows exactly what to say and answers all of the coach's questions with confidence. The example of this fictional character sounds familiar enough; as it turns out, there are many Alvin Macks in the world. Alvin's brain worked just as well as the other students at his college. He was able to process and synthesize information and even to be a leader on the football field, but throughout his life, Alvin's teachers had let him slip through the cracks academically.

Having competed in sports and football via video games (a favorite past-time of many of our black and brown boys and students in general), I know the difficulty of learning and executing plays. Some plays look as complicated as algebraic equations or trigonometry problems. Yet, the athlete masters them. Why is this? How is this possible? It's because the brain is trained to do so. You have to find the way to reach your black and brown boys and train their brains to learn what they need to learn to be successful in the classroom. As stated earlier, they can learn – indeed, they have learned, both for good and bad, and you must now train them to learn what they need to learn in the interest of success in academia and in life.

My mentor Dr. Lorraine Monroe knew that physiologically a brain was simply a brain. There are factors, which affect what we are able to learn and how we process new information. However, we must stick with the basic, fundamental belief that a brain is just a brain. All brains can be taught skills and be trained. When we believe this, we succeed in educating our black and brown boys. When we are born, our brain automatically knows that it must instruct the body to breathe. There is no class on how to breathe; yet, every brain is able to teach the body to do this. Your challenge should be to train your black and brown students' brains in the skills they will need for success and to have their brains grasp these skills as naturally as the skill to breathe.

"Echo excellence; send out greatness

so that it can come back stronger and louder."

JOEL OSTEEN

CHAPTER III
KEEP EXPECTATIONS HIGH — EXPECT THE BEST

Many of you who are teachers probably had parents or loved ones who, from an early age, expected you to go to college. You were expected to be a successful, contributing member of society by someone very close to you, or indeed, possibly many people close to you. Those who expected these things of you helped to guide you along the way and worked to make some things possible or even just easier for you in life. These people were parents, grandparents, aunts, uncles, cousins, coaches, teachers, and friends. Because they expected certain things from you and helped you achieve those things, you have gotten as far as you have in life thus far.

What we must realize as educators is that many of our black and brown boys don't have the network of people we had, and those people in their lives probably don't expect the things that were expected of us. Some of our black and brown boys are not expected to go to college. Some are expected to only make it out of high school. Others are expected to not make it out at all. Some are expected to go to jail and be career criminals. Some are expected to be star athletes and be burdened with bringing their entire families and entourages out of poverty. Some are expected to be star rappers or star performers. Some are expected to be teen fathers or dead-beat dads. And some are expected to amount to, as one of my student's parents put it bluntly, "Not shit, just like their daddy and brothers."

As educators, we must realize that it's our job to expect only the best from all of our black and brown boys. The same things we expect of our children, brothers, and nephews, we must expect from our black and brown boy students. Yes, I know many will come from damaged backgrounds and many will have others outside of school that only expect the worst from and for them. However, we have 6 to 8 hours per day to let them know that we expect the best and won't accept anything but the best from them. When black and brown boys, and children in general, realize they have someone who genuinely won't settle for anything except their best, and that person keeps their expectations of them high, you will be amazed at how hard they will fight to maintain those expectations.

It's very similar to a star athlete who walks onto the court or a field and seems to always perform at a level above the rest even when not performing at their peak. Why? Because they are expected to. They know their fans and coaches expect victory, or at the very least a breathtaking performance. This expectation by others gives that athlete a certain desire or mental edge to do better. Many of the players in the NBA are in the top 5% of basketball players in the world, and they all work very hard, put in years of sacrifice and have natural abilities that the average basketball player doesn't possess. Yet, there is only one Michael Jordan, one Kobe Bryant, and one Lebron James. These players walk onto the court with a certain air of confidence and manage to perform better than the players who are already among the elite in the world. Why? Because they are expected to. We must create this air of confidence for our black and brown boys. We must give them the confidence they need to perform at an elite level by creating plans for success and expecting their best as they execute these plans. We have to set them up to be the best-behaved and highest-performing students.

In the classroom, make it very clear what your academic and behavioral expectations are. Let them know why you expect this and that, despite what others may have expected from them in the past or what others outside of school currently expect of them, you will only expect the best because you know they can give you the best. I have used the examples of Michael Jordan, Kobe Bryant, and Lebron James to students before. I have asked them what they expect from these players whenever they step onto the basketball court. I have also asked why they expect these things. Just about every single time, I get the response "because they are the best." I then make the correlation between what I expect of them in the classroom, at school, and in life is also the best—just like these athletes. I then explain that at one point, these athletes were students just like them. They were once young black boys, students who look just like them; who experienced adversity growing up just like them; and who at some point had a plan devised by someone to help them be the best that they could be. That person expected the best from these top athletes, and you must only expect the best from your black and brown boy students. You will only expect the best because you believe they are the best. They must themselves believe they are the best. If you keep the level of expectation high throughout your time with them, you will soon see how hard your black and brown boy students will work to not disappoint you, and ultimately, to not disappoint themselves.

Expectations as well as classroom and school rules must be made clear from the beginning. There should be no wavering on these expectations and rules. Hold these black and brown boys to the same standards you hold every other student. You will be surprised at how they will oftentimes far exceed your expectations, simply because of your belief in their excellence in the same way that Jordan, Lebron, or Kobe far exceed what is expected of them, and in the process, they awe us.

"Stereotypes of a black male misunderstood,

and it's still all good."

NOTORIOUS BIG

CHAPTER IV

STEREOTYPES KILL — BREAK CYCLES

Some classroom teachers often speak to their student's previous teachers to get information about the student before they have any experience at all with the student himself. For the most part, I disagree with this practice, as it can help to further perpetuate stereotypes and misperceptions. I do agree that at some point you should speak with your colleagues who have a history with that student, but only after you have had a chance to meet and experience the student yourself first. Here is an exercise that I want you to complete in your mind. Below are twelve labels. I want you to close your eyes think of your black and brown boy students and pick a label to put on the front of a t-shirt for each of them:

OVER-
ACHIEVER

UNDER-
ACHIEVER

CLASS CLOWN

SCHOLAR

LEARNING
DISABLED

EMOTIONALLY
DISTURBED

SPECIAL
EDUCATION

SLOW
LEARNER

COLLEGE
BOUND

HIGH SCHOOL
DROP OUT

TEEN
PARENT

PRISON
BOUND

If you imagined any label other than "Over-Achiever," "Scholar," or "College-Bound," then you are already looking at your black and brown boys negatively. These boys live under many negative stereotypes placed on them by society. As educators, we must make certain that we do not help to foster these stereotypes in our classrooms and our schools.

One way in which we kill these stereotypes is to work to only impose positive stereotypes on our black and brown boys. We must view them as scholars and college-bound students from the very beginning. This will allow us to impose positive stereotypes and our expectations upon them from day one. We must remember that these students may have experienced years and years of people imposing negative stereotypes upon them; consequently, at every moment, we must reinforce our positive stereotypes both verbally and through our actions.

Earlier in the chapter, I mentioned that I disapproved of a student's new teacher getting information about the student from the old teacher before the new teacher has a chance to meet the student. I know that in many schools it is customary for the old teacher to give the newer teacher a heads-up about the student, on their work ethic or any other issues that teacher may be aware of. I disagree with this practice, because your black and brown boys may respond differently to you as their teacher or leader. The previous educator may have had any number of experiences, and if you get any information from them before meeting your black or brown boy student, you may already be hindered by the old teacher's stereotypes or experiences. This will impact the positive stereotypes you are now going to have for your black and brown boys.

I am sure that at some point in your life, whether it was as a student or professional, you have experienced one of your classmates or colleagues say that a certain professor is horrid or easy, or that a boss is either tough or lax. I bet there's a good chance that your experience of that person was completely different from what the other person experienced. However, you may have allowed them to put thoughts in your head, and it may have affected your initial view of the person. Sometimes these thoughts keep you from making a fair judgment of a person or a situation. This is something you would never want to do to your black and brown boy students.

You want to keep stereotypes positive and expectations high at all times, especially when initially meeting your students. You don't want anyone else's experiences to taint your views. I believe that once you have had an experience with your black and brown boys (usually towards the end of the first month of school), you should then meet with previous teachers or educators who have also have experience with them. This may help you gather information in order to formulate your plan for success. You must remember to consider all the negative experiences they may have encountered and take very lightly negative stereotypes they may want to mimic to you. You may even have to share with them the fact that you have only the highest expectations of your students and that you wish to impose only positive stereotypes upon them.

We have all experienced stereotypes in some way. Our black and brown boy students face many negative stereotypes every day. We, as educators, must counteract this by giving them only positive stereotypes to live up to. Your black and brown boy students must be scholars, over-achievers, and college-bound in your mind from day one and throughout their educational lives. You must work for the positive in all of your students. Know their shortcomings and push past them. It is amazing when, as a teacher, you see that light bulb finally go off in a kid's head; that smile is worth more to me than any paycheck. You have to work through everything for those small moments of accomplishment, and you build on those small moments to make the complete student.

"It is by choice and not by chances

that we change our circumstances."

NADIA SAHARI

CHAPTER V
TEACH CURRICULUM, NOT CIRCUMSTANCES

My high school basketball coach has a poster in his office of an American Football player on the football field in full gear; however, the player has no legs. Seeing this, I thought, "This is a great Photoshop job." Having played football, I couldn't imagine there being a player with no legs. How wrong was I? I asked my coach, and he explained that not only was the photo real, but this football player was actually good at his craft. He told me the story of Bobby Martin from Ohio – the young man in the photo. I went on to research this athlete. Online, I saw and read countless stories of how relentless and good this guy was. His coach even stated how he was an inspiration to the other players and motivated them to do their best. I imagine his coaches taught him the same plays and made him compete in the same drills as the other players on his team. They did not teach him according to his circumstance, but instead, he was taught the plays and skills (curriculum) he needed to be successful.

I believe if you are an educator reading this book, you have entered into this field to serve and to affect and change lives. We all know that educating others is one of the few careers where there is a major discrepancy between your potential impact on society and the pay you receive. Many of you reading this book have years of teaching experience and both good and bad stories that have affected the way you teach or even approach a student or situation. Having been homeless as a youth and gone through the welfare and shelter system with my single mother, even I can say that I have had to educate students whose circumstances were unimaginable even to me. Had teachers taught to my circumstances and not the curriculum designed to propel me to succeed, I more than likely would not be in a position to write this book. Indeed, I probably would have ended up as a negative statistic.

It's very easy to get caught up in a student's home life and circumstances and feel sorry for them. It is possible to believe that because of these circumstances, they cannot perform at a high level. You may even think if you take it easy on them, they will be better off because they have it so hard in other parts of their lives. In actuality, however, you will be just another person providing a crutch for them and hindering their success. Yes, this may sound harsh and even a bit heartless, but in reality it's better for them. If you show your black and brown boys that just because they are disadvantaged in some areas in life, you'll take it easy on them, you're teaching them the wrong approach to life altogether. Being disadvantaged doesn't mean that they can't accomplish things in life; it just means they may have to work harder. Either way, you have to teach them the same skills you teach all of your students, and in the same manner. Trust me, they will adjust and will appreciate you for it later on.

Think about this. Do you think that on the field or the basketball court, the little guy gets extra breaks from the coaches? Do you think the runt of a gang gets to fall back when it's time for the leader to take them to war? I have personally had the experience of being the shortest guy on the court in many college games, and in preparation for that disadvantage, I felt as if my coaches worked me even harder than they would have if I had been taller. They expected more from me; and I had to prove that I belonged. They didn't teach to the diminutive circumstance that life gave me; they taught me plays, and instilled a certain toughness that allowed the team and me to succeed. So, as a teacher, don't teach to the circumstance of the black or brown boy student who comes from a single-parent home, or has a deadbeat dad or drug-addicted parents, or is even poor or homeless. Teach them the curriculum they need to change these circumstances.

A little while ago, I was watching a program on television. The subject of the program was the rise of John D. Rockefeller, who was at one point one of the richest and most powerful men of his day. Rockefeller still impacts culture today, and his family's wealth and power is among the greatest in the world. It was stated in the program that Rockefeller's father was the equivalent of one of today's dead-beat dads. He was rarely there for Rockefeller during his life, being gone for extended periods of time, and he lived a philandering lifestyle, which included bigamy. His father was very similar to many of the men who are in the lives of some of the black and brown boys we teach. Yet, Rockefeller became one of the richest and most powerful men of his day. All of this was because at some point, someone taught him the curriculum he needed for success, instead of simply teaching to his circumstance.

Shawn Carter (better known as Jay-Z) also grew up without his dad. He fell victim to some of the negative influences that come with being from the Marcy Projects in Brooklyn, NY. Yet, despite his poor upbringing and lack of a father, someone at some point taught him the curriculum he needed to hone his talent and perfect his craft. Not all curriculums are taught in the classroom – some things will be taught out of the context of traditional learning – but they still have to be taught. If the person who helped to hone Jay-Z's skills only taught to his circumstances, then he probably would not be where he is today: one of the wealthiest rappers and most notable performers alive.

Tyler Perry is one of the most influential entertainers of our day. He has risen from a background of molestation and abuse to become a successful actor, director, screenwriter, playwright, producer, author and songwriter. Today, he owns Tyler Perry Movies and Studios and continues to have an impact on acting and filmmaking. He didn't complete school, and at one point was considered homeless. Yet, someone helped to hone his talent and teach him the curriculum he needed to be successful. They could have very easily called him damaged goods and homeless, as I am sure some did. However, at some point, he met someone who didn't do this. He was taught what was needed, and they didn't teach to his circumstances.

Chris Gardner, the subject of the film "Pursuit of Happyness," was raised by an abusive stepfather and was in and out of foster care for much of his life. He was at one point homeless and at the same time trying to raise a son. Despite having had a tumultuous childhood and being homeless, there came a time when someone taught him the curriculum he needed to be a successful millionaire. He relays an incident in which he approached a man who he saw driving a Ferrari. He asked what he did for a living. That man could have easily looked at him, possibly learned of his past, and decided not to speak to him simply because of his circumstances. But he didn't; he helped to teach Gardner the curriculum he needed for success. Gardner subsequently became so successful that he eventually started his own firm and had a movie made of his life starring one of Hollywood's biggest stars, Will Smith.

All of the men mentioned above dealt with circumstances that probably seemed almost impossible to conquer. Many of us probably would not be as successful as they are, if we were given the same life circumstances. They all had a drive, a passion, something in them that motivated them to succeed, but they still needed a teacher. They needed a person to introduce them to and teach them the specific skills that wouldmake them successful. Whether it was in the classroom or in another part of their lives, they were given the curriculum to hone and perfect their skills.

For our black and brown boy students, we have to work on honing and perfecting their skills. We have to teach them the curriculum they need in the classroom and in life so that they can be as successful as possible. Yes, you should care about them, but don't hinder them by providing a crutch. I know it gets challenging to separate caring from hindering, because when you discover some of the things they go through at home, it can be heartbreaking. However, I must implore you to Teach Curriculum, Not Circumstances. Arm them with the knowledge they will need to change those circumstances. Yes, you must be aware of their circumstances, but they shouldn't rule you, what you teach, or how you teach it. Your black and brown boy students must learn and be taught with the same amount of care and rigor that you would teach someone in your own family, despite their circumstances.

"We pay a price when we deprive children of the exposure to the values, principles, and education they need to make them good citizens."

SANDRA DAY O'CONNOR

CHAPTER VI
EXPOSURE, EXPOSURE, EXPOSURE - BROADEN THEIR HORIZONS

I once listened to a sermon by Joel Osteen wherein he said, "Destination disease is contagious." He then explained how those who you hang out with can be helpful or harmful to you. We all see how, in a classroom, there is often a kid or even a group of kids who mislead otherwise good students. The "bad kid" or the "class clown" can disrupt a lesson to no end. Oftentimes, our black and brown boys come from situations where their surroundings can seemingly determine their destination. They may come from neighborhoods where there aren't many men in their households and there aren't many positive role models. They may come from neighborhoods where the people they see have lived there, and only been there, forever, never traveling or experiencing the wonders of life outside of their neighborhood.

I remember when I was growing up, walking through Harlem to school in the mornings. I would pass by corner after corner, seeing some of the same men in the morning that I would see on my way home from school many hours later, still loitering on those same corners. I often wondered what they did for a living and how they were able to survive doing the same thing day after day. Many of our black and brown boys will be exposed to gangs, violence, and never-ending cycles of drugs and abuse, and we must find a way to counteract this by exposing them to the more positive things in life so that they can become more than just the men that hang out on the corner.

Many people, and statistics for that matter, would like for us to believe that our black and brown boys' "destinations" have already been set. They would like for us to believe that many will end up on the same corners I used to walk by every day. They would like for us to believe that these boys cannot become productive, contributing members of society. They would like for us to believe that these boys are more likely to go to prison than to go to college.

I know if you are reading this book, you don't believe this. You believe that our black and brown boys' destinations are set by what they learn and how they use it. This means that we must teach them all we know and more. We must expose them to things that are different than what they see in their daily lives.

As educators, we know that the more to which we are exposed, the more our minds begin to explore different possibilities. If all we know is one thing or one way of living, then the odds of us ever really wanting to know or do anything more are slim. There is a reason you can walk into any classroom in any inner-city school, ask a group of black and brown boys what they want to be when they grow up, and receive more or less the same answer. It doesn't matter if you are in Harlem, NYC, Atlanta, GA, or Chicago, IL. Most of the responses you will get will be positions in the sports and entertainment industries, and they will most likely be those who compete or perform in those fields, as opposed to owners, managers or agents. Why is this? We are living in a time where virtually any information or any knowledge we need is at our fingertips instantly. We can learn about anything, see photos of things we aspire for, and even follow people through social media in their daily lives on our smartphones or computers. Yet, it appears that sports and entertainment are what our black and brown boys are exposed to, and subsequently, aspire to.

Is it that they feel there will be more fame and glory if they are in front of the camera or performing? Is it that they see the lives many athletes and entertainers make for themselves, and they yearn for that livelihood for themselves and their families? It's debatable. However, I will say this. The more our black and brown boys are exposed to, the more they can aspire to be. I remember my fourth grade teacher, Ms. Weissberger, used to take our class on many different field trips. We were just a group of 9- and 10-year-old kids from Harlem, and she gave us the chance to travel to museums throughout the city and to learn and be exposed to things we otherwise would not have been. Every year, we took a trip to Chinatown, and it was on one of these trips that I used chopsticks for the first time. I remember bringing my chopsticks home so that I could try to teach my mother how to use them. Ms. Weissberger also exposed us to different careers and industries. We met doctors at the hospital, lawyers in the courtroom, firemen at the fire station, policemen at the police station, and even accountants in their offices. This may sound simple, but to a group of kids growing up in Harlem in the late 1980s, these were experiences that none of our friends at other public schools experienced.

Ms. Weissberger knew that opening up our minds and exposing us to different careers provided life choices for us. I cannot tell you how many times my answer changed as to what I wanted to be when I grew up, but my answers were always much different than those of my friends who had not been afforded the same opportunities. She also knew that exposing us to different cuisines and areas of the city would allow us to realize that there was much more to the world than the crack-infested neighborhoods we lived in. She even exposed all of the boys in her class to different sports. We all played tennis. While most of our friends only knew basketball, football, and baseball, we knew tennis. As a youth from Harlem heading to tennis camps, many doors were opened, which broadened my horizons significantly. Tennis is a sport I play to this day, and I even played competitively while in college.

My exposure to all of these different experiences continued throughout high school. I attended one of the first college preparatory schools in Harlem, and it prepared me not only academically as a student, but as a person as well. The leaders and teachers there knew their black and brown boy students not only had to know how to read, write, think, and compute, but they also had to be able to smoothly and comfortably fit into society. This public school had teachers who taught not just their black and brown boys, but all of their students learned entrepreneurial skills, proper grooming, and etiquette. They exposed us to the Opera, Broadway shows, and things that we would otherwise not have been able to see or do. They knew how invaluable these things would ultimately be for us.

What does this look like for your black and brown boys? What does not having set limits really mean for their lives? How do you begin to have them understand that their current lives and neighborhoods do not have to be their ultimate destinations? How do you get them to even want to see that they can be much more than what others say or even what they themselves think they can become? I would start by exposing them to as much as you can right away. Broaden their horizons. No matter what city or town you live in, I am sure there is much they can see and experience that will be entirely new to them. Expose them to new careers, new delicacies, different sports, the theater and fine arts. As meaningless or as corny as some of these things might seem to them now, those experiences last a lifetime. Don't assume they are aware or have already been exposed to any given experience. Just think about it. I learned to use chopsticks in fourth grade. My mother had never used chopsticks. I taught her. Something that is simple or even mundane to us can impact our black and brown boys and others in their lives in a dramatic and meaningful way.

I was talking to a group of young black and brown boys one day, and I asked each of them what they wanted to be when they grew up. Out of 19 of them, there were 11 aspiring professional athletes, six aspiring music stars and actors, one music producer, and one lawyer. The lawyer stated that he would represent all of them. Now, I never want to tell any kid what they can or cannot be, especially if they say they wish to become something. So, I challenged them. I asked each of them to name one person in the field they wanted to work in as an adult, and I asked them to tell me what they thought their typical day would look like. Keep in mind, these were a group of boys ages 11 to 13, so they envisioned much of their day to be leisure and fun activities. I then further challenged them by having each of them research what it took for a person to enter the field to which they were aspiring. They had to find out how much education they needed to get into that field and how much a person in that field made per year on average. Additionally, I had them come up with a budget. Next, they had to tell me if that person had a boss, manager, agent, owner, or anyone they had to answer to other than fans, since most of them stated that they wanted to be in the entertainment or sports fields. They then had to tell me, if there was a higher boss or manager, and how much people in those positions made.

After my little exercise, I began to have them examine different career fields in each of the industries they chose, from the obvious to the not-so-obvious. I did this in order to show them how many different people and jobs surrounded and supported that one person that they mentioned earlier. This not only helped to open their eyes and answer many misconceptions they had about their dream careers, but it also exposed them to other careers and paths as alternatives. At the end of the exercise, the one boy who stated that he would be a lawyer for all of the athletes and entertainers in the group now said that he would much rather be a lawyer for the team and for record-label owners. He recognized that this was where the real money was. He was such an entrepreneur, and a little exposure may ultimately bring him much further than he ever anticipated.

So what can you do? You have to expose your black and brown boys to as much as you can, from academics, to careers, to sports, to the WORLD. They should know that their current situation is not their end destination.

"I never ran my train off the track,

and I never lost a passenger."

HARRIET TUBMAN

CHAPTER VII
TRAIN TO GIVE BACK —
THE HARRIET TUBMAN
DISEASE

W hen we as educators teach about Harriet Tubman, we mostly go through the basics of what she accomplished: her escape from slavery and subsequent use of the Underground Railroad, returning many times to free others. For the purposes of this book and for our black and brown boys, I want us to examine what she did through a more focused lens. She not only was a slave who escaped to freedom, which was something that could have cost her life, but she went back many times to the dangerous areas of the country, where slavery was legal, and rescued many more slaves. She gave back and helped others even after she had already helped herself.

I believe as a good educator, you will do many of the things in this book (among many other techniques) to help create black and brown boys that will become educated, productive members of society. But is that your end goal? Is your goal to educate a classroom of black and brown boys, or is it to change the lives of the many black and brown boys to come? If you train your black and brown boys to have the "Harriet Tubman Disease," they will be consumed with not only "making it," but also reaching back to help others. If you help them to get infected with this disease, you will help to affect the lives of more black and brown boys than you can imagine.

Ironically (or maybe not so ironically), just before I wrote this chapter, I ran into my fourth grade teacher, Ms. Weissberger, who I mentioned in a previous chapter. I was visiting my old elementary school to look at the teaching practices and tone of the charter school, which now occupied its space. I had no idea that I would see anyone who taught me while I was there, but the security guard told me she was in the library with the new principal of the school. I met Ms. Weissberger in the library and I introduced her to a colleague with whom I was traveling. Her eyes glowed with accomplishment when she found out that I was an administrator at a charter school in the South Bronx. She was a woman who did all she could to educate her black and brown boy students. She helped many of us to accomplish great things. When she saw I was infected with the "Harriet Tubman Disease," it was as if she realized the true purpose of her life's work. She knew I was one of her brightest students and that I could have ended up in any career and been successful, but the fact that I work to educate black and brown boys in some of the poorer neighborhoods of New York City and help to change their lives is all because she instilled that "give-back" disease in me.

We see this on many occasions when an athlete or a pop star visits their old neighborhoods or schools. They often tell students that, if they made it, then anyone can make it. We also see this on the career days that take place periodically in schools across the country. Why do they do this? Why do people give of their time? I have participated in career days and can personally say that I am in my field because I want to see young minds grow. I feel that, for these same minds, there are endless possibilities. I want to motivate not just black and brown boys but all students to be their best and to realize that education is the foundation of success.

How do we get our black and brown boys to want to give back once we have equipped them with the skills to be successful? It is my belief that we first have to instill in them the importance of giving back, even before they have officially "made it." You need to expose them to volunteer opportunities while they are still your students, help them to buy-in on changing their communities. Have them realize that, even as youth, they can have an impact. Provide them with leadership and volunteer opportunities. They should feel as though every accomplishment they have would be more gratifying if they were able to help someone else. Challenge your black and brown boys to give back, challenge them to be leaders, and challenge them to use their success as a springboard to help others.

There is a reason many successful private schools don't fold. They understand the importance of the "Harriet Tubman Disease." They know that the stronger their alumni network is, the more sustainability and longevity their school will have. They not only have donors who create large endowments, but they provide networks where students get internships, where doors can be opened with access to the people and things that will help them in the future. There are some elite private high schools whose endowments are larger than many colleges. They give away more money in scholarships than some urban schools have to spend on their entire budgets. The alumni of and donors to these schools realize the importance of giving back and providing opportunities. Why should our black and brown boys not learn the importance of this? They don't have to wait until they become the rich athlete or the successful lawyer or doctor. You can teach them and begin to ingrain these ideas in them today.

I call this idea the "Harriet Tubman Disease," because the desire to give back should consume them the way a disease consumes your body and mind. We should want our black and brown boys to be consumed with the idea of giving back, so they can help many more black and brown boys move forward.

I was once at a conference and heard a speaker say, "Because I am, I know that you can become." Once we help to push our black and brown boys to become successful, we need to have them help others become as or more successful even than they are. It is only then that we will begin to see the kind of impact we can have as educators as many black and brown boys continue to be successful for generations to come.

"I am not a creator, what I do is discover and uncover. When I uncover, the boys themselves discover qualities within themselves that they didn't even know they had. My job is to take the spark and fan it, when it starts to become a little flame I feed it, and I feed the fire until it becomes a roaring blaze and then when it becomes a roaring blaze I put huge logs on it, then you really got a fire going."

CUS D'AMATO

CHAPTER VIII

DON'T LET THEM QUIT – COACH LIKE CUS D'AMATO

ron Mike Tyson is arguably one of the most famous boxers of all time. He is also arguably the most feared man to ever put on boxing gloves. He was the youngest heavyweight champion in boxing history to date. He is also known for, during the height of his boxing career, for not being what you might call the best role model. He admitted to charges of abuse, drug use, and intimidation outside of the ring. However, for the purpose of this book, I would like to use Tyson and his famous trainer as an example of potential that was cultivated and realized in the ring.

The late Cus D'Amato was a boxing trainer who trained hall-of-fame fighters. If you ask me, he was a teacher at heart. He understood a key principle that he used to help young boys discover and uncover talent they had within. He was there to hone and nurture that talent. One of his pupils went on to become the face of boxing for a generation and made hundreds of millions of dollars. He took a street kid from one of the poorest neighborhoods in Brooklyn, NY and created a multi-millionaire. He took a kid who ended up in a youth detention facility in upstate New York and turned him into a trendsetter and a sports figure the nation couldn't keep its eyes off. He took a kid that looks like many of the black and brown boys in your classrooms and not only changed history but created it.

As I watched interviews of Mike Tyson talking about Cus D'Amato, I realized a few things. First, Tyson's life changed drastically when Cus died. This is the beginning of when we start to see his antics outside of the ring begin to overshadow his boxing accomplishments. Second, he had a high regard for Cus D'Amato, and used only terms of endearment whenever he spoke of him. Third, he gave Mike such confidence in his abilities and made Mike believe in himself even when he didn't want to or know how to. I will paraphrase what Mike says in one interview. He stated that Cus would often say that becoming the world champ and knocking people out was what he was supposed to do. He was not supposed to jump up and down or celebrate when he won a match; it was merely what was expected of him. In the classroom, you should celebrate wins both big and small, but your black and brown boys should be expected to succeed because of the work and preparation you both go through.

I remember entering middle school and hearing for the first time that we were all going to college. I had good teachers in my primary-school years, but this was the first time every adult around me simply expected all of us to go to college. It was shocking at first; it was as if a new language was being spoken around me. After a while, however, we all began to really believe and could conceive that we were going to college. College and college preparation became a daily part of our vocabulary and shaped many of our daily educational routines. I think this is part of the reason why many charter schools use college names and have collegiate themes for their advisory classes. They are ingraining into these students the idea that college is an expectation that students must realize.

As a teacher, you must also ingrain in your black and brown boys' brains the idea that college and success are expectations that have to be realized in a way very similar to the way that Cus D'Amato ingrained in Mike Tyson's head the idea that he would be the Heavyweight Boxing Champion of the World. In one interview, Mike Tyson said that in order for him to be successful in the ring, he had to look at himself as something greater than he actually was at the time. He knew that many of his opponents were bigger, more talented, and more experienced than he was. His trainer helped to build up his confidence so much that he was able to go up against fighters against whom he ought to have lost – and win. Of course, this is easier done when you have prepared for it. So, prepare your black and brown boys to be successful and practice the skills they need for success over and over. Have it become second nature so that when they have to compete against students who have more resources or who come from more economically advantaged backgrounds, they feel overconfident in knowing that they belong and they will succeed.

Cus D'Amato understood that, as a teacher, you have to enhance and build on the skills that are already there – skills that your students may not even know they have. Your job is to help them to discover what's already inside of them. In one interview, Mike Tyson recalls how Cus would always complement him. He would continually tell him how great he was or how good of a job he was doing. Mike didn't understand until later that Cus was building up his confidence so that he could become great. He told him over and over and over again that he could be champion of the world – and one day Mike realized that he could be, and then he was. But it took Cus D'Amato's belief in him, along with the skills he imparted, for it to dawn on Mike that he had to believe in himself. It got to the point where even when Mike wanted to quit, the reassurance and continued belief and support from Cus helped him to persevere.

The simple truth is that most people won't reach their full potential without someone to believe in them. Believe in your black and brown boys. Show them you believe by preparing them and constantly reminding them of their end goal. Give them the confidence they need every day.

"It always seems impossible until it's done."

NELSON MANDELA

CONCLUSION

I despise when I hear an educator say, "Well, they just can't read" or "They just can't get it" when speaking of any demographic. When it comes to our black and brown boys, this angers me even more, because it shows how certain educators will just give up. My simple response is "If they can't read, then teach them; if they don't get it, then come up with a different way to help them understand."

Our black and brown boys learn many different things and have many different skills. There are many examples of black and brown boys who turn into black and brown men who excel in life. If they can remember and write a rap song, then they can write, read and recall. If they can remember dance steps or execute difficult plays, then they can compute and synthesize information. We just have to work on ourselves as educators to learn more effective ways to relate to and teach our black and brown boys.

WE MUST: CARE, motivate, expect the best, break stereotypes and train them in the skills they need for success; expose them to the wonders of the world; instruct them on the importance of giving back; save them from the naysayers; save them from themselves; save them from their environment – SAVE THEM.

I was once listening to a motivational speaker who was sharing the story of the Chinese Bamboo Tree. I was amazed at how diligent and patient one has to be to plant and care for this tree before it grows. It is a very tedious and repetitive process. Unlike most other plants and trees, Chinese Bamboo is quite unique. When this bamboo is planted, watered, and nurtured for the first year, it does not grow, not even an inch. The second year, the third year, even the fourth year you must continue to irrigate, fertilize and care for the bamboo tree and yet nothing happens – it fails to sprout. During the fifth year, "the magic happens". All of the persistent hard work finally seems to pays off, the tree sprouts upwards of 80 feet in as little as six weeks.

The biggest thing to ponder is does this amazing growth happen the six little weeks that we can see above ground as this tree sprouts upwards or is the growth truly happening during the years of consistent watering and nurturing? The answer should be obvious, that it's the years and years of consistency which helped to grow the roots underground, roots that would support a tree that sprouts so high and fast.

The motivational speaker said four things which stood out to me:

1. You have to first plant a dream

2. You have to do the daily things that would make your dream a reality

3. You have to ignore those who may say your dream may not happen

4. You have to push pass your own fear and doubt and keep taking action even when it seems like there are no results

This is a great story for us as teachers, educators or anyone who deals with the black and brown boy demographic. Change will not come instantly; it will take time, practice and consistency. If you remain diligent and consistent you will get results. You have to fight through even when these changes may not be seen right away or it may seem as though change will never come. Because, like the Chinese Bamboo tree after consistent practice and vested time you will get amazing results. You should also share the story of the Chinese Bamboo tree with your black and brown boys. They should know that it will take practice and consistency over a period of time before they may see results with issues they are working on. It may take a while for them to develop a particular skill, or learn to master a particular subject, but consistency and diligence will pay off.

Maybe there IS a magic wand that you can wave over all of your students and suddenly have excellent classroom management. I have yet to find one, and I believe you've probably read this book because you haven't found one either. However, hopefully you have found some strategies that will assist you in becoming a better educator and leader of black and brown boys. I truly hope you now see that you educate and train your black and brown boy students the same way you educate all of your students – because, really, IT'S NOT ROCKET SCIENCE.

To contact the author for more information visit:

www.natehiggins.org

CPSIA information can be obtained at www.ICGtesting.com
Printed in the USA
BVOW05*0931220115

384380BV00007B/4/P